THE MEXICAN AMERICANS

THE MEXICAN AMERICANS

Julie Catalano

CHELSEA HOUSE PUBLISHERS

New York   New Haven   Philadelphia

Senior Designer: Laurie Jewell
Designers: Noreen M. Lamb, Louise Lippin
Cover Illustration: Paul Biniasz
Banner Design: Hrana L. Janto

First Printing
1 3 5 7 9 8 6 4 2

Library of Congress Cataloging in Publication Data

Catalano, Julie.
  The Mexican Americans.
  (The Peoples of North America)
  Bibliography: p.
  Includes index.
  Summary: Discusses the history, culture, and religion of the Mexicans, factors encouraging their emigration, and their acceptance as an ethnic group in North America.

  1. Mexican Americans. 2. Mexico—Emigration and immigration. 3. United States—Emigration and immigration. [1. Mexican Americans. 2. Mexico—Emigration and immigration. 3. United States—Emigration and immigration] I. Title. II. Series.
E184.M5C375 1988   973'.046872073   87-893

ISBN 0-87754-857-9

CONTENTS

A
NATION
OF
NATIONS

Daniel Patrick Moynihan

T he Constitution of the United States begins: "We the People of the United States . . ." Yet, as we know, the United States is not made up of a single group of people. It is made up of many peoples. Immigrants from Europe, Asia, Africa, and Central and South America settled in North America seeking a new life filled with opportunities unavailable in their homeland. Coming from many nations, they forged one nation and made it their own. More than 100 years ago, Walt Whitman expressed this perception of America as a melting pot: "Here is not merely a nation, but a teeming Nation of nations."

Although the ingenuity and acts of courage of these immigrants, our ancestors, shaped the North American way of life, we sometimes take their contributions for granted. This fine series, *The Peoples of North America,* examines the experiences and contributions of the immigrants and how these contributions determined the future of the United States and Canada.

Immigrants did not abandon their ethnic traditions when they reached the shores of North America. Each ethnic group had its own customs and traditions, and each brought different experiences, accomplishments, skills, values, styles of dress, and tastes in food that lingered long after its arrival. Yet this profusion of differences created a singularity, or bond, among the immigrants.

The United States and Canada are unusual in this respect. Whereas religious and ethnic differences have sparked intolerance throughout the rest of the world—from the 17th-century religious wars to the 19th-century nationalist movements in Europe to the near extermination of the Jewish people under Nazi Germany—North Americans have struggled to learn how to respect each other's differences and live in harmony.

Millions of immigrants from scores of homelands brought diversity to our continent. In a mass migration, some 12 million immigrants passed through the waiting rooms of New York's Ellis Island; thousands more came to the West Coast. At first, these immigrants were welcomed because labor was needed to meet the demands of the Industrial Age. Soon, however, the new immigrants faced the prejudice of earlier immigrants who saw them as a burden on the economy. Legislation was passed to limit immigration. The Chinese Exclusion Act of 1882 was among the first laws closing the doors to the promise of America. The Japanese were also effectively excluded by this law. In 1924, Congress set immigration quotas on a country-by-country basis.

Such prejudices might have triggered war, as they did in Europe, but North Americans chose negotiation and compromise, instead. This determination to resolve differences peacefully has been the hallmark of the peoples of North America.

The remarkable ability of Americans to live together as one people was seriously threatened by the issue of slavery. It was a symptom of growing intolerance in the world. Thousands of settlers from the British Isles had arrived in the colonies as indentured servants, agreeing to work for a specified number of years on farms or as apprentices in return for passage to America and room and board. When the first Africans arrived in the then-British colonies during the 17th century, some colonists thought that they too should be treated as indentured servants. Eventually, the question of whether the Africans should be viewed as indentured, like the English, or as slaves who could be owned for life, was considered in a Maryland court. The court's calamitous decree held that blacks were slaves bound to lifelong servitude, and so were their children. America went through a time of moral examination and civil war before it finally freed African slaves and their descendants. The principle that all people are created equal had faced its greatest challenge and survived.

Yet the court ruling that set blacks apart from other races fanned flames of discrimination that burned long after slavery was abolished—and that still flicker today. The concept of racism had existed for centuries in countries throughout the world. For instance, when the Manchus conquered China in the 13th century, they decreed that Chinese and Manchus could not intermarry. To impress their superiority on the conquered Chinese, the Manchus ordered all Chinese men to wear their hair in a long braid called a queue.

By the 19th century, some intellectuals took up the banner of racism, citing Charles Darwin. Darwin's scientific studies hypothesized that highly evolved animals were dominant over other animals. Some advocates of this theory applied it to humans, asserting that certain races were more highly evolved than others and thus were superior.

This philosophy served as the basis for a new form of discrimination, not only against nonwhite people but also against various ethnic groups. Asians faced harsh discrimination and were depicted by popular 19th-century newspaper cartoonists as depraved, degenerate, and deficient in intelligence. When the Irish flooded American cities to escape the famine in Ireland, the cartoonists caricatured the typical "Paddy" (a common term for Irish immigrants) as an apelike creature with jutting jaw and sloping forehead.

By the 20th century, racism and ethnic prejudice had given rise to virulent theories of a Northern European master race. When Adolf Hitler came to power in Germany in 1933, he popularized the notion of Aryan supremacy. "Aryan," a term referring to the Indo-European races, was applied to so-called superior physical characteristics such as blond hair, blue eyes, and delicate facial features. Anyone with darker and heavier features was considered inferior. Buttressed by these theories, the German Nazi state from 1933 to 1945 set out to destroy European Jews, along with Poles, Russians, and other groups considered inferior. It nearly succeeded. Millions of these people were exterminated.

The tragedies brought on by ethnic and racial intolerance throughout the world demonstrate the importance of North America's efforts to create a society free of prejudice and inequality.

A relatively recent example of the New World's desire to resolve ethnic friction nonviolently is the solution the Canadians found to a conflict between two ethnic groups. A long-standing dispute as to whether Canadian culture was properly English or French resurfaced in the mid-1960s, dividing the peoples of the French-speaking Quebec Province from those of the English-speaking provinces. Relations grew tense, then bitter, then violent. The Royal Commission on Bilingualism and Biculturalism was established to study the growing crisis and to propose measures to ease the tensions. As a result of the commission's recommendations, all official documents and statements from the national government's capital at Ottawa are now issued in both French and English, and bilingual education is encouraged.

The year 1980 marked a coming of age for the United States's ethnic heritage. For the first time, the U.S. Census asked people about their ethnic background. Americans chose from more than 100 groups, including French Basque, Spanish Basque, French Canadian, Afro-American, Peruvian, Armenian, Chinese, and Japanese. The ethnic group with the largest response was English (49.6 million). More than 100 million Americans claimed ancestors from the British Isles, which includes England, Ireland, Wales, and Scotland. There were almost as many Germans (49.2 million) as English. The Irish-American population (40.2 million) was third, but the next largest ethnic group, the Afro-Americans, was a distant fourth (21 million). There was a sizable group of French ancestry (13 million), as well as of Italian (12 million). Poles, Dutch, Swedes, Norwegians, and Russians followed. These groups, and other smaller ones, represent the wondrous profusion of ethnic influences in North America.

Canada, too, has learned more about the diversity of its population. Studies conducted during the French/English conflict determined that Canadians were descended from Ukrainians, Germans, Italians, Chinese, Japanese, native Indians, and Eskimos, among others. Canada found it had no ethnic majority, although nearly half of its immigrant population had come from the British Isles. Canada, like the United States, is a land of immigrants for whom mutual tolerance is a matter of reason as well as principle.

The people of North America are the descendants of one of the greatest migrations in history. And that migration is not over. Koreans, Vietnamese, Nicaraguans, Cubans, and many others are heading for the shores of North America in large numbers. This mix of cultures shapes every aspect of our lives. To understand ourselves, we must know something about our diverse ethnic ancestry. Nothing so defines the North American nations as the motto on the Great Seal of the United States: *E Pluribus Unum*—Out of Many, One.

A Mexican plantation owner and his wife tour their hacienda in 1834.

FROM MAJORITY TO MINORITY

The Mexican-American story begins in the 1500s, when Spain conquered Mexico and its people. Mining and agriculture lured the Spaniards farther north, into the area that is now the southwestern United States. The colonization that followed transplanted many Mexican Indians and *mestizos* (people of European and Mexican-Indian ancestry) because it relied on their labor.

Spain managed to retain control of Mexico and the northern frontier until 1821, the year Mexico won its independence. But in 1848 Mexico lost the northern half of its territory (including California, Arizona, Utah, and Nevada) to the United States. When this happened, the Mexicans living in the territory were given the choice of becoming citizens of the United States or returning to Mexico. Many 20th-century Mexican Americans are descendants of those who chose to remain.

Since then the driving force behind Mexican immigration to the United States has been the availability of work. When the U.S. economy grew and the Mexican economy faltered in the late 19th century, thousands of Mexicans crossed the border to work as ranch and field hands. They were encouraged by U.S. farmers and ranchers who needed cheap labor. Mining and railroad work lured thousands more. As the United States moved into the industrial age, many Mexicans found work in its factories. Today, Mexicans continue to cross the U.S.-Mexico border at a steady rate. Many enter legally; many resort to other means; but they all come in search of work, opportunity, and the American dream.

An essential part of the American dream for thousands of Mexicans entering the United States each year is the freedom to retain their heritage while gaining a new future. The sentiments of Mexican-American author Richard Rodriguez express this freedom:

> I am not so sure what it means to be a Mexican. I am related to my Mexican ancestry in tone, in gesture, in style. But meanwhile, I have to assert my Americanism, too. You and I, we share the same American air. I have to assert that Abraham Lincoln is my cultural godfather. I have to say that I am more indebted to Jefferson than to Zapata. I am indebted to Walt Disney. Even if I had been taught only in the Spanish language, I would still have to be a part of this culture and to

Entire Mexican families often immigrated to the United States in search of work.

know who Farrah Fawcett is. That is why most Hispanics simply become Americans. America is a place where you don't lose your culture—you gain one.

   The Mexican Americans' heritage is complex. In essence, it is a many-layered blend of cultures and includes their original national identity as well as that of Spanish and Anglo colonists. ✸

For decades all of Santa Fe has turned out to celebrate the city's annual fiesta.

An engraving from a 16th-century European history book depicts Indians laying their treasures at the feet of conquering Spaniards.

A TWICE-CONQUERED PEOPLE

During the 15th century Mexico was an isolated land populated by various Indian tribes. But by the 1500s the Aztec Indians had gained control of central and southern Mexico by conquering and subjugating many of the indigenous tribes of the region.

The Aztecs, who called themselves "Mexica," created a rich and powerful empire. They built pyramids, aqueducts, palatial homes, parks, and zoos. They were accomplished artists, astronomers, engineers, and architects. This thriving civilization soon fell prey to Spanish explorers who were looking for new lands to conquer.

When the Aztec chief Montezuma (1480–1520) was notified of approaching ships, he sent his emissaries to meet them. A centuries-old legend had predicted the arrival of Quetzalcoatl, the fair-skinned and bearded serpent god. According to this legend, Quetzalcoatl had been banished from

Aztec mastery of architecture is exemplified by the Great Temple of Tenochtitlán.

Mexico after being defeated by the warrior god. But before he left, Quetzalcoatl promised the people that he would return. Thus, when the Spaniards arrived in the same year that Quetzalcoatl was expected, the Aztecs thought the god had honored his promise. Montezuma sent his emissaries to appease the gods by giving them gold and other treasures, hoping Quetzalcoatl would leave them in peace. But this gesture only served to tantalize the Spanish sailors, evoking images of great wealth. The gifts spawned tales of magnificent Aztec riches, and the Spanish explorers, particularly Hernán Cortés (1485–1547), became determined to claim the territory for the Spanish Crown.

At first the Indians thought that Cortés and his troops were gods and tried to defeat them with witchcraft, but soon they were overpowered by the invaders' military sophistication. Even though his troops were greatly outnumbered, Cortés conquered Mexico rapidly. The Indians hesitated to attack when they saw soldiers mounted on horses, animals unknown in Mexico.

The Spaniards had other advantages, too. For example, their weapons were much more advanced than those of the Aztecs. Also, the various Mexican-Indian tribes who had escaped Aztec domination were eager to support the Spaniards. Thus, in 1521, Cortés gained control of Tenochtitlán, the Aztec capital, and claimed Mexico for the Spanish Crown.

Under Spanish control, a new social structure emerged. The *peninsulares* (native-born Spaniards) were at the top of the caste system, followed by the *criollos*, or Creoles (Spaniards born in New

The corn god was one of many Aztec deities.

19

Spain). At the bottom of the system were the Africans who had accompanied the Spanish on their exploration of the Western world, and the Mexican Indians. This social structure created a captive labor force for the development of New Spain.

Colonization

Because religion and government were intertwined in Spanish society, the conquerors' first step toward colonization was an effort to convert the Indians in New Spain to Roman Catholicism. Several factors simplified this conversion process. First, the Indians viewed their gods' failure to avenge the Spaniards' destruction of Indian temples and idols as a divine acceptance of conquest. Second, the Indians were able to equate the saints of Roman Catholicism with their own lesser gods. Although many of the Indians converted, they actually practiced a religion that was a hybrid of Roman Catholicism and their own.

This 16th-century Aztec drawing portrays Cortéz's cruel treatment of the Indians.

Conversion was not the Church's only focus. The clergy also founded schools and hospitals and taught the Indians better farming methods and new ways of weaving cloth and making pottery. Although Spanish and Indian cultures began to merge, the relationship between the two remained unequal.

As emissaries of the Crown in Mexico, the clergy had to create a labor force—and the Mexican Indians met its general requirements. The Church profited greatly at the Indians' expense, robbing them of their identity in the process. This captive labor force had to build and live in villages called *congregaciones*, dress in European clothes, practice a new religion, learn a new language, pay tribute to the Spanish Crown, and support the community through farming.

The Church was not alone in its exploitation of the Mexican Indians. Spain encouraged further

Franciscan friars were a mainstay of Spanish colonial life.

Settlers in the New World craved the goods provided by colonial traders.

colonization by granting conquerors and settlers who had served the country well the right to Mexican-Indian labor. Under a system of colonization known as the *encomienda*, the settlers, *encomenderos*, were supposed to provide the workers with food, clothing, shelter, and health care. However, they did not fulfill their obligation, and the Indians were no better off than slaves. The captors worked the Indians beyond their capacity.

In 1541 Indian outrage at Spanish control and the abuses of the encomienda system erupted in the Mixtón War, an unsuccessful revolt. By 1549 some in the religious community had pressured

Spain into rescinding the encomenderos' right to Indian labor, but a new system, called *repartimiento*, soon surfaced to replace it. This system turned out to be even more brutal because no one was responsible for the Indians' welfare. Indians were assigned to work for a specified amount of time on projects that the Crown deemed essential. In return for their labor, the Indians were supposed to be paid wages, fed, and housed by the colonists. Instead, the colonists mistreated the Indians and failed to pay them.

Over the course of the 16th century, the combination of mistreatment and European diseases obliterated more than two-thirds of the Mexican-Indian population. Their labor had enabled the Spanish to appropriate their land; by 1535 what had once been an Aztec empire was christened "New Spain." Although Indians still constituted the majority of New Spain's population, a new caste of people, known as mestizos, was emerging. These people of mixed Indian and Spanish blood— the ancestors of today's Mexican Americans—became the primary labor force behind the next phase of Spain's Mexican colonization efforts.

Northward Expansion

A lack of food, the desire for greater fortune, and the push to expand Spain's territory in the New World soon drove the colonists farther north. Franciscan and Jesuit priests led this migration to the area that is now bounded by Nebraska to the north, Texas to the east, and California to the west, building missions that extended Spain's power.

The missions provided the colonists with their social and recreational life. But the primary goal of the missions was to establish and defend territorial claims for the Crown from attacks by North American Indians. Spanish civilians joined the clergy in its attempts to conquer and colonize the northern territories. They settled in a fanlike pattern, creating small, defensible communities in strategic valleys and fertile river areas. The majority of the Mexicans living in the four principal settlements—today's New Mexico, California, Texas, and Arizona—were mestizos and Indians.

Throughout most of the 17th century, life on the frontier was riddled with hardship. A lack of labor paralyzed mining efforts, and cattle and sheep overgrazed the lands. The settlers who survived were moved to supposedly self-sufficient rural estates known as *haciendas*, but they often lacked services and goods. Occasionally, traders and merchants would carry their wares north from the Mexican state of Chihuahua, but their prices were too high for the colonists. As a result, the traders came less frequently, forcing the colonists to make what they needed or barter for it. But they still needed the services of doctors, carpenters, and blacksmiths.

Spain, itself in a state of economic collapse, offered its troubled colonists little help; in fact, the government caused them further hardship by outlawing trade with foreign countries and banning immigration to the colony. But these laws backfired. Because the colonists could not afford to trade with the mother country, their only option was to develop black-market trade with foreigners.

In the 18th century, Spain's Bourbon dynasty reorganized the colonies. Despite positive administrative changes, a new fiscal system, and the revitalization of mining and agriculture, the settlers' problems were not yet resolved. As mining and agriculture began to thrive, native-born criollos came to resent Spain's economic and political control and to push for Mexican independence.

Mexican Independence

A sequence of revolts lasting from 1810 to 1821 paved the way for Mexican independence. In 1810 a Mexican priest named Miguel Hidalgo y Costilla (1753–1811) led a rebellion of Indians and groups

Revolutionary priest Miguel Hidalgo y Costilla was executed by royalist forces in 1811.

President Antonio López de Santa Anna commanded his countrymen during Mexico's war against the United States.

of mixed ancestry. In his speech "El Grito de Dolores" ("The Cry of Dolores")—named for the city in which it was delivered—Hidalgo made demands for a new government. Although Hidalgo became a casualty of this rebellion, another priest, José María Morelos y Pavon (1765–1815), took over the revolution, calling for the redistribution of land. This rebellion and others against Spanish rule continued for several years.

Finally, unable to suppress the growing discontent, Spain proposed a plan for independence in 1821. The plan appealed to thousands of Mexicans, but Spanish royalists (those loyal to the Crown) found it unacceptable. Later that year, Mexico won its independence under the leadership of Augustin de Iturbide (1783–1824). A conservative, de Iturbide guaranteed the independence of the Church and forestalled the opposition of powerful bishops. The colonists tolerated this hierarchy until, determined to break further with Spain, they ousted the bishop's friars in 1835 and sent the mission system into decline.

While Mexico was fighting for independence from Spain, both countries had virtually ignored the northern territories. Mexico's loss of influence in the region was inevitable. The relatively small Mexican population in the north was distributed throughout a vast area that Mexico's centralized and weak postindependence government could not control. Merchants and trappers from the United States were able to establish a stronghold in the territory, adding another cultural influence to regional life. Their ways clashed with those of the natives. The Mexicans perceived these merchants

The Santa Barbara mission still stands as a reminder of California's colonial heritage.

and trappers as crude, coarse, and violent people who killed—animals or people—for pleasure. The Mexicans, in contrast, were formal and reserved.

But the Anglos (white people of non-Hispanic descent) regarded the Mexicans as a backward people in a backward land. Because the Anglos did not understand the Mexican culture or language, they assumed a position of superiority just as the Spanish had when they conquered the Aztec Empire. As the Anglo population grew, so did its political and economic control. The concerned Mexican government soon retracted its open invitation to foreigners and instituted new laws to hinder foreign trade. But the settlers were not about to give up their newfound luxuries. Antonio López de Santa Anna (1794–1876), Mexico's president, was forced to rescind the laws. Mexico's control of its northern territory was endangered.

Texas Revolution

By the 1830s approximately 30,000 Americans were living in Texas, outnumbering the Mexican residents by nearly 6 to 1. This imbalance was partially the result of a land grant that the Mexican government had once issued to lure Anglo settlers to the area. Both the Mexican and Anglo Texans now hungered for self-determination for Texas.

The Mexican government had adopted a democratic system of self-governing states controlled by a central authority. This system united Texas with two old Spanish provinces to create one state. Texans repeatedly petitioned the Mexican government to grant them independent statehood, but their requests were ignored. Hostility grew, and by 1832 trouble was brewing in Texas as Anglo and

Mexican Texans joined forces to rebel against the Mexican government.

The first skirmishes of the Texas Revolution took place in 1835, when Texans captured a Mexican customs garrison. A few months later, they seized a supply garrison. On December 5 Texan armies took over the Alamo Mission, and San Antonio, the chief city of Texas, fell to the Texas rebels. Santa Anna considered this rebellion a personal insult and took retaliatory action. His troops killed the nearly 200 Texans who were barricaded behind the Alamo Mission walls. Feeling victorious, Santa Anna and his troops made the fatal decision to retreat and rest, unaware that the Texan forces of famed American general Sam Houston (1793–1863) were closing in behind them. The battle was over quickly, but this time the Texans were victorious. More than 600 Mexican soldiers were killed in the Battle of San Jacinto (April 21, 1836),

Known as the "cradle of Texas liberty," the Alamo is a symbol of freedom for all Americans.

Military Plaza, now the site of San Antonio's city hall, was a commercial center in the 1880s.

whereas only 9 Texans lost their lives, and Texas became an independent republic. Mexico was losing its foothold in the northern territories.

The United States Prevails

During Mexico's fight for independence, the Anglo presence in Mexican territory had grown considerably. For example, Kentucky mountain men had traveled west to take advantage of the rich trapping trade. They also played a primary role in the development of the major trade routes. Many Anglo trailblazers set their sights on California. They became Mexican citizens, married into California's prominent families, and assimilated into Mexican society. In the 1840s, news of California's wealth and magnificence lured increasing numbers of Americans from the East Coast. California soon became the focus of the United States's belief in its Manifest Destiny—that it was meant to possess the continent from shore to shore. This penetration of Mexican territory created a collage of diverse cultures. For the most part the blending process was peaceful until a new area of conflict arose.

By the early 19th century, hostility between abolitionists and slaveowners divided the United States. The South and the North were both eager to bring like-minded new states into the Union, thereby tipping the scale in their favor. The pro-slavery South looked to the independent Republic of Texas, where, two decades earlier, slavery had been instituted in defiance of Mexican law. When the U.S. House of Representatives offered the Republic of Texas statehood in 1845, Texas accepted. The Mexicans who stayed in the republic when it joined the Union became the first sizable group of Mexicans living in the United States.

The Spoils of War

Mexico refused to acknowledge Texas's U.S. statehood; it had never even ratified the treaty that recognized Texas's independence. Still, the Mexican government did not think that losing the territory was reason enough to go to war. But then American settlers in Mexican-controlled California staged an armed bid for independence—the Bear Flag Revolt of 1846. This new territorial skirmish aggravated the tensions between the neighboring countries. Finally, another 1846 border disagreement led them into war.

The Mexican War was relatively short. Within a year, Mexico had lost nearly one half of its territory to the United States—including what are now the states of California, Nevada, Utah, New Mexico, Colorado, Wyoming, and parts of Arizona. The U.S. government assumed responsibility for the thousands of Mexicans living in its new territory. It gave the residents the choice of becoming U.S. citizens or returning to Mexico. Those who stayed (approximately 80 percent) became the first official Mexican Americans.

The First Become the Last

Three factors influenced the United States's reshaping of the former Mexican territories: the separation of Mexican Americans from their land, cultural hostility between Mexicans and Anglos, and economic development that relegated Mexican Americans to positions as low-paid laborers. Although Mexicans still outnumbered Anglos in most areas of the Southwest, the newly empowered white minority began to subdue the majority through discriminatory practices. The whites took land from the Mexicans, usurped their political power, and threatened their social position. Anglo Americans desperately tried to create a white-dominated society, and tensions between Anglos and Mexican Americans escalated. Even though the Treaty of Guadelupe Hidalgo, which was signed at the end of the Mexican War, guaranteed the right of Mexican Americans to retain their property, language, religion, culture, and customs, these rights continued to be violated.

Some towns passed ordinances outlawing Mexican *fiestas* (festivals). English became the official language of the new U.S. territory, putting the Mexicans at a greater disadvantage. Most laws were written only in English, and it was even against the law to testify in court in Spanish. Most teachers spoke only English, and many forbade schoolchildren to speak Spanish in the classroom. Segregated restaurants, stores, and cemeteries became the

(continued on page 41)

IMAGES OF PROGRESS

Many centuries before it was colonized by Spain, Mexico evolved a complex culture preserved today through archeological finds such as these pre-Columbian treasures—a Bat God with outthrust tongue and a female statuette.

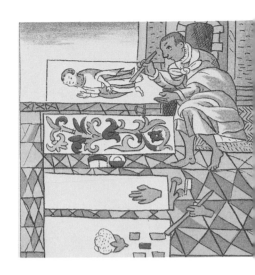

Spanish conquerors brought their native religion and culture to Mexico, as shown in this 16th-century illustration of a robed monk, and below, in an anonymous 19th-century oil painting that contrasts colonial aristocrats, perched on a stone wall, with the rocky cliffs of Guanajuato.

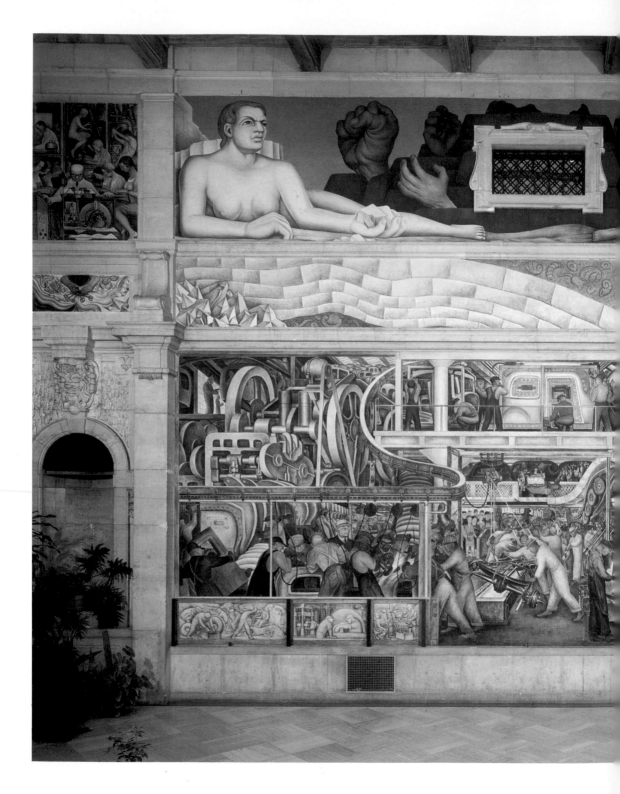

Mexican muralists are legendary, none more so than Diego Rivera, whose massive fresco honoring American auto workers, commissioned during the Great Depression, fills an entire room in the Detroit Institute of Arts.

A community art form, murals serve as unifying landmarks in diverse neighborhoods such as this one in New York City, and often involve teamwork, as shown below by a pair of artists working together.

Labor, a major subject of Mexican-American art, is central to the experience of many Mexican Americans, as attested by this workers' rally in southern California and by farmhands who toil in the Southwestern heat.

The collective gains won by labor unions such as the United Farm Workers and the United Auto Workers have bettered conditions in the fields and factories that employ many Mexican Americans.

(continued from page 32)

norm. In effect, the Mexicans entered another period of second-class citizenship—this time at the hands of Anglo Americans. This occurred although the Mexicans had been in North America long before the Anglos.

In Texas the economy depended on cattle ranching, which meant that wealth and power were based on the ownership of livestock and land. After Texas joined the Union, Anglos gained control of most of the Mexicans' land through court battles. (During the early period of Spanish colonization, the Spaniards had settled on land that they had taken from the North American Indian tribes. Spain, and later Mexico, usually gave this land to the settlers through land grants that did not stand

Mexican laborers pose for a group photograph at the turn of the century.

During the early 1900s Anglo mineral miners depended on the labor of Mexicans but paid them meager wages.

up in the American judicial system.) Stripped of their land, the Mexicans had no choice but to work at menial jobs. The only exception occurred in the trading towns that developed along the Rio Grande. There, trade activities required the ability to speak Spanish, putting Mexicans at an advantage. Thus, a Mexican middle class evolved. However, this situation was not the norm. By 1890, the labor-intensive nature of Texas's growing cotton industry had relegated the majority of the state's Mexican population to the status of the laborer.

In New Mexico Spanish-speaking residents of different classes intermarried and created a diverse community that frequently mixed with Anglos and dealt with them as equals. This equality disintegrated, however, when agriculture and immigration problems set in. Years of excessive grazing by horses and cattle had depleted the land of its mineral supply, impeding new growth. In addition a continuous stream of poor Mexicans migrated north from Texas in search of work and flooded the labor market. The strained economy worsened relations between Mexicans and Anglos. As the Anglo population increased, the work force became segregated, and Mexicans were once again shunted into servile roles.

The rapidly growing Anglo population in California (enticed by the gold mines) changed the complexion of this predominantly Mexican region. Mexicans and Anglos had coexisted in peace until greed and prejudice led the Anglos to tax, lynch, rob, or expel Mexican miners. When the gold mines dried up and the fervor subsided, Anglos migrated south. Many settled in Los Angeles, a large Mexican settlement founded by Franciscan priests in 1771, and the surrounding region as California developed an agriculturally based economy. Although Mexicans had owned most of the land in Southern California, a devastating flood in 1862 and the prolonged drought that followed wiped out their wealth. By the 1880s, Mexican Americans in California had lost all political ground and were landless. Like their counterparts in Texas and New Mexico, they were disfranchised by new Anglo settlers. These descendants of the powerful Aztecs found they were once again the victims of colonial expansionism. ∾

FROM
ACROSS THE
BORDER

As the Mexican population in the United States lost ground, the southwestern economy soared, luring new immigrants from south of the border. During this period, from the 1860s through the turn of the century, Mexico vacillated between phases of revolution and political stability. These fluctuations in the political climate adversely affected the region's economy and migration to the southwestern United States increased.

U.S. census figures indicate a surge in the total Mexican-American population from approximately 75,000 in 1890 to an estimated 562,000 in 1900. Although the immigrants represented all levels of Mexican society, the majority were poor and illiterate. Thus, they joined their compatriots as a captive labor force for southwestern agriculture and other labor-intensive industries.

For example, the burgeoning railroad industry relied heavily on Mexican labor. This industry depended initially on Chinese workers in 1882 but lost them when Congress limited Chinese immigration. The railroads were in dire need of a new

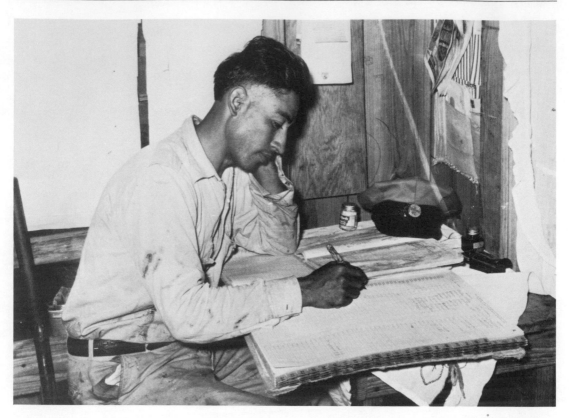

A Texas labor contractor calculates his profits in 1939.

labor source to complete the monumental task of laying track through the rugged southwestern terrain. By 1908, the Southern Pacific and Santa Fe railroads were hiring more than 1,000 Mexican workers per month from both sides of the border. Eventually, 70 percent of the railroad's track-laying crews and 90 percent of its maintenance crews were Mexican.

The mining industries in Colorado and Arizona also relied heavily on Mexican workers, for prospecting as well as for brute strength. Mexicans discovered the famous New Almaden quicksilver mine near San Jose, California, and unlocked many of the West's silver and gold resources.

In agriculture, the scientific and technological advances that paved the way for reservoir construction, field irrigation, and year-round farming also increased the demands for cheap labor. Anglo farmers recruited Mexican labor to pick, process, pack, and ship their growing yields. Many laborers were hired by contractors who recruited, supervised, and paid the workers. But this system often led to abuse. Labor contractors would withhold payment and provide only the most miserable living conditions in order to increase their profits. Mexico's economy was so poor that Mexicans would not risk the loss of their jobs or worse, deportation, by rebelling against these conditions.

Although the northward flow of Mexicans was constant, these migrations were small compared to those that were to follow. Social, political, and economic upheavals in both the United States and Mexico were soon to set the stage for major Mexican migrations.

The Great Migration

Mexican emigration peaked during the 1920s as the U.S. economy flourished and the demand for unskilled labor grew. Immigration laws that restricted Asian and Eastern European immigration created a void in the labor force, and the Mexicans were readily accessible. Thus, between 1920 and 1929, approximately 600,000 Mexicans entered the United States on permanent visas, which granted them legal residence without U.S. citizenship. These Mexicans remained citizens of their native country and were restricted to contract work in the agricultural sector. (Even the majority of Mexicans who remained in the United States and became

American citizens after the Mexican War were confined to menial labor, particularly on farms and in the mines.) The majority settled in the Southwest, once again, primarily in Texas and California.

Illegal Aliens

In addition to the legal immigrants, thousands of Mexicans crossed the borders illegally to fill the labor gap of the early 1900s. At the peak of Mexican immigration, in 1924, the United States established the Border Patrol in an effort to prevent unlawful entry. But the attempt proved futile.

Mexicans who wanted to avoid bureaucratic delays and visa expenses found ways to cross the poorly guarded 2,000-mile border. They were often aided by American employers who wanted a steady supply of low-cost labor for their farms and industries. Some employers hired professional smugglers who forged documents to bring in illegal immigrants. The smugglers, termed *coyotes*, turned the workers over to an *enganchista*, or labor contractor. Occasionally, employers would report illegal immigrants to immigration officials after the work was done and before the wages were paid. As illegal immigrants, the Mexicans had no legal recourse.

World War I

At the outbreak of World War I, President Woodrow Wilson (1856–1924) called on Americans to increase U.S. manufacturing and agricultural production to meet wartime needs. However, as thousands of young men marched off to war, workers once again became scarce. Future U.S. president Herbert Hoover (1874–1964), then head of the U.S. Food Administration, asked the Department of Labor to ease the restriction that limited migrants to agricultural work. As a result, many Mexicans began to enter skilled professions as machinists, upholsterers, bookbinders, and mechanics.

Because industry held the promise of wages that were higher than those offered by agriculture, it drew large groups of Mexican Americans to midwestern and northern cities. For example, Chicago soon had the largest Mexican population of any city outside the southwestern United States. An increasing number of Mexican Americans found em-

Nonunion workers shell pecans by hand during the Southern Pecan Shelling Company strike of 1938.

Jobless Mexican Americans join other victims of depression unemployment in a 1931 Los Angeles hunger march.

ployment in the automobile factories of Detroit; the tanneries and meat-packing plants of Gary, Indiana; and the steel mills of such states as Ohio and Pennsylvania.

Tales of these opportunities encouraged further Mexican immigration. A popular Mexican *corrido*, or ballad, echoed the feelings of the many Mexicans who left their homeland to find work:

> Good-bye my beloved land,
> Now I am going away,
> I go to the United States
> Where I intend to work.

By 1929, the number of Mexican-born people living in the United States was estimated at 1 million. But economic factors soon brought Mexican immigration to a halt.

Repatriation

The stock market crash of October 1929 shattered America's economy and ushered in the Great Depression. As the industrial bubble burst, millions of workers were displaced. The Mexican-American population was particularly vulnerable because it was already at the lower end of the economic ladder. Many Mexicans were forced out of their jobs in favor of unemployed Anglos. In the months that followed, approximately 85,000 Mexicans, victims of a poor economy and discrimination, left the United States. Those who remained found themselves in competition for scarce jobs with Anglo Americans, who turned against them even more vehemently. State and local governments began campaigns to remove illegal aliens, hoping that this action would create more jobs for American citizens.

The situation became particularly hostile in Southern California, where federal and local authorities subjected Spanish-speaking people to daily harassment and detention. (Similar treatment was given to citizens who were suspected of being illegal aliens because of their appearance and language.) Although few illegal aliens were actually apprehended, the fear of deportation led approximately 75,000 Mexicans to leave the region.

Purged from their jobs, many Mexican Americans became dependent on government aid. Suddenly, other Americans began to view them as a liability. Their earlier contributions to industry and agriculture were forgotten. The same work force that had been eagerly recruited in the 1920s was regarded with disdain in the 1930s. To recover some of its displaced work force, the Mexican government cooperated with American authorities who wanted to return Mexico's former citizens. This process was called *repatriation*. Many Mexicans were offered free train rides back to Mexico. But the repatriation movement soon surpassed Mexico's ability to absorb the returnees.

Nearly 500,000 people of Mexican descent moved to Mexico during this time. Most were from the Southwest, but others left homes in Illinois, Michigan, Indiana, and Minnesota. Still, repatriation merely shifted mass unemployment from one country to another. As the depression wore on, fewer Mexicans left. They were determined to endure the rough times, and U.S. president Franklin Roosevelt's New Deal programs provided hope that steady employment was on the horizon.

The Bracero Program

Although it had deported Mexican workers just a decade earlier, during the 1940s the United States asked Mexico to fill the labor shortage inflicted by World War II. In 1942 the countries negotiated an agreement whereby Mexico would supply contract workers, known as *braceros* (hired hands). Thousands of Mexicans came to the United States on temporary visas. The Mexican Americans who had stayed in the United States during the repatriation program now had to compete with the Mexican braceros, who worked for lower wages. The new labor force displaced many Mexican-American workers, driving them from such areas as central and southern Texas to other states.

The original bracero program operated from 1942 to 1947 and on a less formal basis from 1947 to 1964. In 1944, at the peak of World War II, agents brought 62,170 braceros into the United States. The postwar bracero movement reached its peak in 1956, when 500,000 contract workers arrived to work on farms in 28 states. During the course of the bracero program, about 5 million Mexican nationals gained entry as seasonal work-

During the Great Depression, Mexican Americans often lost their jobs to Anglos and were forced to depend on government aid.

*Labor contractors often
provided squalid housing for
migrant workers.*

ers. The braceros received work assignments and
meager wages and lived in substandard housing.
When a job was finished they were sent back to
Mexico.

One goal of the bracero program was to reduce
the number of illegal aliens by providing a means
for Mexicans to earn wages without allowing them
to become permanent residents. The inadequately
funded Border Patrol had been ineffective. *Moja-
dos*, or wetbacks (so called because they commonly
swam the Rio Grande, in order to gain entry into
the United States), could easily slip across the border. To discourage the illegal flow of migrants,
Congress strengthened the laws against transport-
ing aliens in a 1954 campaign known as "Operation

Wetback." Within 5 years, 3.8 million illegal aliens had been expelled from the United States.

The Mexican and U.S. governments extended the bracero program even though it was meant to be a wartime emergency measure. In fact, during most of its existence, the bracero program had nothing to do with a wartime labor shortage. It was a way for American agriculture to take advantage of Mexico's economic hardships. Inadvertently, the program fostered a large volume of undocumented migration to the United States. ∾

Striking field laborers of the 1930s were forerunners of today's United Farm Workers.

THE STRENGTH OF A PEOPLE

Because the majority of Mexican immigrants who came to America seeking employment tended to be the poorest and least educated Mexicans, many Anglos assumed that all Mexicans were poor and uneducated. And so an ethnic stereotype evolved. Mexican Americans also faced the blanket discrimination leveled at almost all non-whites.

Racial and cultural stereotypes are often based on the intentional misinterpretations one group makes of another. For example, during the Texas Rebellion, Anglos developed the notion that Mexicans were cowards because a small band of Texan rebels defeated an overwhelming number of Mexican troops. The Anglos seemed to forget that many of those brave Texas rebels were Mexican Texans. Mexican Americans were slow to react to the stereotypes created by the Anglos. One reason for this was that the Anglo- and Mexican-American worlds were separated geographically, linguistically, and socially.

An example of the danger to Mexicans of stereotyping by the Anglos is the Sleepy Lagoon case. One August day in 1942, the body of José Díaz was found near the Sleepy Lagoon swimming hole in Los Angeles. The police used this incident to put an end to the street gangs that populated the barrios by arresting 300 Mexican-American youths who belonged to a local gang. Seventeen of the twenty-two youths placed on trial for the murder of Díaz were convicted of crimes ranging from first-degree murder to assault, even though there were no witnesses. Anti-Mexican prejudice riddled the trial.

In the fall of 1943, the Sleepy Lagoon Defense Committee started raising money to appeal the court's decision. A higher court reversed the decision a year later because of the lack of evidence. However, this reversal ignited an outburst of anti-Mexican sentiment and led to Los Angeles's Zoot Suit Riots (so named because of the popularity of this fashion among young Mexican Americans). U.S. servicemen attacked Mexican Americans on the street and dragged them out of public places. Youths began to form gangs for protection, and it became apparent that police attitudes were contributing to the problems in the barrio. One police lieutenant offered the following rationale for the gang crimes: "Crime is a matter of race, and the tendency to commit crimes can be inherited. Therefore, the race must be punished."

A History of Protest and Progress

World War II provided a major turning point in the lives of Mexican Americans. Between 350,000 and 500,000 Mexican Americans fought beside their Anglo neighbors in World War II and became one of the most decorated ethnic groups, eventually receiving 39 Congressional Medals of Honor. Many Mexican-American veterans used the G.I. Bill to finance college educations and trade and technical schooling. Many of those who did not serve in the armed forces found jobs in industries that had previously been closed to them. As this new world began to open up, a new awareness of discrimination surfaced, making Mexican Americans more eager than ever for justice. Yet despite the broadening of their world, they realized that the resources for such a struggle could be found only within their own community.

Historically, Mexican Americans were at the forefront of the labor reform movement as early as the 19th century. In 1883 Mexican-American cowboys led a strike for higher wages against powerful cattle companies in Texas. A decade later, Mexican-American miners fought the dual-wage system that paid Anglos more than their Mexican-American co-workers.

Fruit pickers in California join a protest against exploitative growers in 1933.

Hispanic workers harvest broccoli on a Florida farm.

In the 20th century Mexican Americans continued to participate in the labor reform movement. In 1913 they protested the living conditions on the Durst hop ranch near Wheatland, California. The riot that ensued led to a general awareness of the plight of migratory workers and is considered a landmark in the history of farm labor unions.

During the 1920s, California workers organized the Confederación de Uniones Obreras Mexicanos (CUOM), or Confederation of Unions of Mexican Workers. They registered about 3,000 workers and created 20 local chapters in California. The union led a historic strike in 1928 against the Imperial Valley melon farmers and became a training ground for future labor leaders. The strikes and protests that followed proved to the growers that the Mexican labor force was not as docile as they had imagined.

César Chávez

Labor reform for migrant workers culminated in the revolutionary movement led by César Chávez (b. 1927), whose policy of protest through non-violence made this son of migrant farm workers the Chicano counterpart of the black civil rights leader Martin Luther King, Jr. In 1952 Chávez joined a California community services association and began organizing wine-grape pickers, first locally and then statewide. Ten years later he founded the National Farm Workers Association, forerunner of the powerful United Farm Workers Union.

Chávez drew thousands of grape pickers into his movement, and by using strikes, fasts, and marches, showed them that collectively they could bargain with owners and growers for better wages. In 1965 Chávez led grape pickers on a historic 300-mile march from their hometown of Delano to the state capital at Sacramento. Three years later, building on his reputation, he won wide support for a national boycott of U.S. table grapes. Soon the movement had gained enough momentum to include California's vegetable pickers and Florida's citrus workers. Chávez, a man of courage and charisma, defied the growers and became a hero to Mexican Americans.

The Chicano Movement

An important effect of Chávez's union was renewed ethnic pride among Mexican Americans. In the late 1950s a parallel force arose, the *Chicano* Movement (also known as *El Movimento*). The word *Chicano*, originally a racist slur applied to Americans of Mexican descent, was claimed and used proudly by two of the movement's leaders, Reies López "Pete" Tijerina (b. 1926) and Rodolfo "Corky" Gonzáles (b. 1928).

At first, supporters worked within the system by forming alternative political organizations, but some found the influence they desired slow in coming, and so they became more radical. In the 1960s López Tijerina organized an effort to regain the lands that had been granted to the Chicanos' ancestors by the Spanish and Mexican governments. The first action of the Alianza Federal de Mercedes (Alliance of Land Grants) was the 1966 occupation of Echo Amphitheater—part of a national forest and an old New Mexico land grant. The Alianza declared the area a free state and set up a provisional government. They arrested two forest rangers for trespassing on the newly declared territory, conducted a trial, and gave them suspended sentences. López Tijerina was convicted on assault charges for this incident and sentenced to a two-year prison term and five years' probation. He was released in 1971 under the provision that he break contact with the Alianza (which by then had formally disbanded).

César Chávez captures media attention during a strike against the Chiquita Banana company.

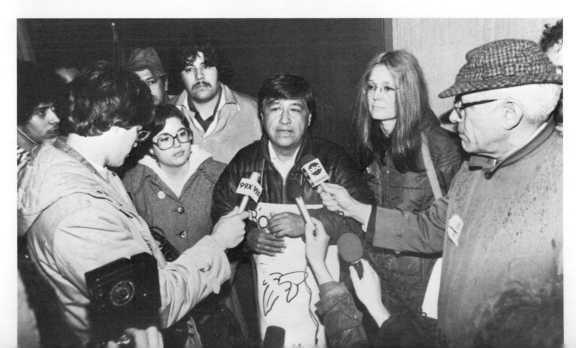

Political Power

Radical groups such as the Alianza did not attract the majority of Mexican Americans who wanted social and economic change. Most sought instead to increase Chicano representation in local, state, and national government, feeling that they needed greater access to the mainstream of American politics. Mexican Americans defined several key goals, including persuading non-Hispanic candidates to consider the needs of the Mexican-American community; organizing large-scale voter registration and community organization drives; and supporting the passage of legislation to undo past injustices to the Hispanic population. Traditionally, Mexican Americans have worked through the political bi-party system or such groups as the Mexican American Political Association and the Political Association of Spanish Speaking Organizations.

In 1974 two Mexican Americans were elected governor—Jerry Apodaca in New Mexico and Raúl Castro in Arizona. They were the first Chicano governors to be elected since Ezequiel C. de Vaca and Octaviano Larrazolo served as governors of New Mexico in the early 1900s.

In the 1976 presidential election, Mexican Americans were responsible for Jimmy Carter's significant margin of votes in both Texas and Ohio. More recently, in an attempt to sway the traditionally Democratic Hispanic vote (81 percent for Carter in 1976), the Republicans have created a Republican National Hispanic Assembly that rivals the Democrats' Hispanic Affairs Division. Mayor Henry Cisneros of San Antonio, Texas, Toney Anaya, former governor of New Mexico, and Linda Chávez, former assistant to President Reagan and

Jerry Apodaca served as governor of New Mexico from 1975 to 1979.

Mexican-American parents attend a Parent Teacher Association meeting in New Mexico in 1943.

director of the Office of Public Liaison, are just a few of the Mexican Americans continuing the tradition of political action in the 1980s.

Educational Organizations

Nowhere has the political reform work of Mexican Americans been more active than in the field of education. Most Mexican immigrants believed that one of the best ways to get ahead was through education. Yet public schools consistently neglected the needs of Spanish-speaking students and migrant families. The Chicano community has worked hard to reverse this situation. The best-known Mexican-American educational organization is the League of United Latin American Citizens (LULAC), which was formed in the Texas Rio Grande Valley in 1929. Its original agenda was to inform the community about the social, political, and economic rights and duties of the Mexican Americans. After World War II the organization worked to end school segregation. Still active today, its membership exceeds 200,000.

The Chicano Movement also fought for educational improvements, including a reduction in school dropout rates, the development of bilingual and bicultural programs, expanded scholarship and support services, and the creation of Mexican-American studies programs. Such student organizations as Movimiento Estudiantil Chicano de Aztlán (Chicano Student Movement of Aztlán) have also been at the forefront of the fight for educational reform.

The original charter of the Mexican American Legal Defense and Education Fund (MALDEF), which was founded in 1968, was to protect the legal rights of Chicanos and to provide educational assistance grants to Chicano lawyers who would work to achieve the organization's goals. Since its inception MALDEF has been a leading force in advocating educational opportunities for Americans whose primary language is not English and in developing employment and training opportunities for them. Its members, such as activist Antonia Hernández, also wage an ongoing campaign to ensure that minorities have adequate resources. Without bilingual education, young Mexican Americans sometimes feel lost between two languages and two cultures. As one Chicano put it concisely:

> When I was in school, the teachers beat me if I spoke Spanish. They wanted to remind me that I was an American. After school, my friends beat me if I spoke English. They wanted to remind me that I was a Mexican.

Hernández and other educational reformers extend the long tradition of Mexican Americans who have organized to erase cultural stereotypes and to demand better working and learning conditions for their people. ∾

Toney Anaya, New Mexico's governor from 1982 to 1986, is an influential member of the Democratic party.

*Santa Fe natives pose in traditional
Mexican costumes during the city's
1928 fiesta.*

A CELEBRATION OF COMMUNITY

Like other ethnic groups in America that have faced discriminatory practices and economic oppression, Mexican Americans have drawn on the strength of the family as a defense against a demanding, indifferent, often hostile society. The family is the essential preserver of Mexican-American customs and culture. The Mexican-American definition of immediate family traditionally includes grandparents, aunts, uncles, and cousins, related either by blood or marriage.

But no support system can insulate an ethnic group from changes that occur within the society at large, including a shift in traditional roles taken by men and women. The changing economy of the 19th century marked the entry of Mexican-American women into the labor force. As the men lost their jobs, women were forced to seek work as domestics, laundry and garment workers, and farm laborers. Modern influences—such as assimilation into an American way of life, education, and geographical mobility—have created new roles for men and women.

Several generations of the Salas family pose proudly for a photographer.

First-generation Mexican Americans worked long hours, usually at menial jobs, so that they could afford to educate their children and thus provide a better life for them. As second- and third-generation Mexican Americans improved their status, their means of providing traditional family support changed as well. A successful Mexican-American lawyer who was a child when his parents immigrated to the United States in the 1960s says

How we take care of our families is a measure of how well we are doing. It's simply the same tradition manifested in a new way. Now, we establish trust funds for our children, invest in stocks and bonds, provide subsidies, real estate, or retirement income for our parents. It comes from the same motivation and the same source of pride. We still take care of our own.

Certainly, some customs have been lost along the way. For example, traditional Mexican styles of dress are worn only at street festivals, and elements of folk religion now are found only in folk remedies. Many traditions reappear during times of celebration, especially holidays.

Fiesta Time

Catholicism has played a significant role in the life of Mexican Americans. For instance, Chicanos rejoice during Navidad (Christmas), when the religious significance of the holiday blends with colorful and rousing fiestas. The fiestas are occasions for dancing, singing, and recounting tales, such as the one about a land of plenty where tortillas grow on trees and anyone who works gets a whipping. Blindfolded children squeal as the brightly colored *piñata* is raised. Each one stands beneath this brightly colored pottery jar filled with candy, fruits, and gifts and then swings a stick into the air, trying to break the piñata and scatter its treats on the ground.

Many Mexican women carefully tend sacred objects that express their religious faith.

The Christmas ritual of *Las Posadas* (The Lodgings) is still celebrated in many Mexican-American communities. Reenacting the Holy Family's search for a place to stay, participants go from house to house in a song-filled, candlelit procession. At first they are refused admittance, then they are joyfully welcomed into the homes and given a party, complete with piñata, Mexican hot chocolate, *pan dulce* (sweet bread), cookies, and guitar-strumming musicians.

Many southwestern towns and cities host their own versions of Las Posadas and other Christmas celebrations. In San Antonio, for example, a three-day Christmas festival called Fiesta Navidena is held in *El Mercado* (the market). These festivals would not be complete without folk dancers in authentic and colorful costumes, traditional Christmas foods, and the arrival of "Pancho Claus" for the children. Another traditional holiday event, the Blessing of the Animals ceremony, symbolizes the significance the animals had on the night Christ was born.

Sometimes the fiesta spirit captures a whole city. In San Antonio, where more than half of the population is Hispanic (Spanish-speaking), fiestas often erupt spontaneously. For example, when a developer decided to move a historic hotel rather than demolish it, thousands of Hispanics and Anglos declared an instant fiesta.

Not all fiestas are spontaneous, however. The preparation for San Antonio's annual 10-day fiesta begins as soon as the last one has ended. This celebration, which commemorates the 1836 revolution against Mexico, is a southwestern version of the New Orleans Mardi Gras. Women parade in multicolored Mexican dresses and men don *guayaberas* (fanciful shirts that are tucked in front while the tails trail behind). The entire town takes on the atmosphere of a *cantina* (saloon), and barges filled with flowers jam the narrow San Antonio River.

Historical Holidays

In addition to celebrating traditional American holidays many Mexican Americans annually observe two special dates in Mexico's history. The more important of these is Diez y Seis, which celebrates Father Miguel Hidalgo's El Grito de Dolores speech, delivered September 16, 1810 outside

his parish church in the town of Dolores, in Guanajuato. It marked the beginning of Mexico's long struggle for independence. The other holiday, Cinco de Mayo (the 5th of May), commemorates Benito Juarez's defeat of French forces at the city of Pueblo in 1862. In cities with large Mexican-American populations, such as Los Angeles and San Antonio, festivities often include parades with bands, floats, and men in *charro* (Mexican horsemen) costumes. These national holidays help Mexican Americans celebrate their homeland's long journey from colony to modern statehood.

The River Parade is one of the most popular events of the San Antonio fiesta.

Cultures Converge

Although some older Mexican-American traditions have faded, new ones surface as the Mexican and American cultures continue to converge. For example, Mexican corridos, or ballads written for guitar and voice, can be heard throughout the Southwest. These songs usually describe either the adventures of Mexican heroes or the experience of the common people. Recently, historians have begun to record these ballads to preserve Mexican-American history. *Mariachi* music, another traditional Mexican musical form, blends the sounds of brass and strings.

One of the first Mexican-American musical phenomena, Tex-Mex music (also known as *musica nortena*), was inspired by Mexican-American encounters with the German Americans in New Braunfels, Texas, in the early 1900s. The Mexican Americans added their unique instrumentation to the German polka rhythm and Tex-Mex *polkeros* evolved, featuring the accordion and bass. More contemporary Tex-Mex groups use drums, horns, and electric instruments and combine influences from jazz, rock, and country and western music. Although Tex-Mex music was originally instrumental, it now often includes lyrics that portray the Mexican experience.

Dance troupes keep Mexican folk culture alive. The *jalisco* is a dance of courtship that dates back

Tex-Mex band members rehearse for a performance in a Santa Fe hotel around 1940.

to the 1700s. The Mexican polka was considered the dance of Mexican aristocracy until it spread to the peasants of Mexico and the Texas border. Dance has also been incorporated in Mexican-American theater.

But perhaps the element of Mexican culture most prevalent in the United States is its cuisine. Tacos, tostadas, enchiladas, and tamales are on the menus of restaurants and fast food chains in every region of North America. Many grocery stores now carry Mexican spices and other ingredients once considered exotic, so that everyone can experience the diversity of Mexican cuisine. Mexican food is much more than a burrito, taco, and enchilada combination plate. Other dishes feature ingredients such as cilantro, tomatillos, Mexican cheeses, and chillies combined with meats and fruits.

The popularity of Mexican restaurants in the United States has coincidentally introduced Anglos to other elements of Mexican culture. Many non-Hispanics now furnish their homes with Mexican folk art, paintings, woodwork, pottery, and sculpture. And the merging of cultures continues on a much larger scale. Today nearly a dozen major cities, including Chicago, San Antonio, and Los Angeles, are virtually bilingual. Spanish translations often appear on English street signs, in public service messages, and on billboards, further testifying to the cultural convergence. ∾

Mexican chefs often use unusual combinations of ingredients, such as chicken and unsweetened chocolate, to prepare native dishes.

INDIVIDUAL EXCELLENCE

Profiles of the numerous Mexican Americans who have made impressive contributions to business and industry, the arts, government, education, and entertainment would fill volumes. The following few represent some of the many outstanding individuals who have opened the door to justice, opportunity, and recognition.

Joseph Montoya (1915–1978), descendant of one of New Mexico's oldest families, was the youngest man ever elected to New Mexico's state legislature; in 1964 he became the first Mexican American elected to the U.S. Senate. In 1969 he and Senator Edward Kennedy established the Cabinet Committee on Opportunities for the Spanish Speaking. The committee sponsored conferences on education and employment, provided an employment aid service, analyzed community needs, and ensured that federal programs reached the Spanish-speaking population. In addition to championing bilingual education, Montoya campaigned to resolve the problems of the American Indian community.

In 1953 Henry B. González (b. 1916) was elected to the Texas state senate, becoming the first Mexican American to be seated in that body in 110 years. In his words, González stands for "classless, raceless politics" and takes a moderate approach to winning civil rights and equality for Mexican Americans. He played a key role in defeating the bracero program. More recently, González secured educational benefits for Hispanic Vietnam War veterans.

In 1970 Patrick F. Flores (b. 1929) became the first Mexican-American bishop appointed to the U.S. hierarchy of the Roman Catholic church. In 1972, Bishop Flores helped establish the Mexican American Cultural Center in San Antonio; he also founded the National Foundation for Mexican American Vocations and the National Hispanic Scholarship Fund. At a rally to secure collective bargaining rights for meat packers and clothing and machine workers, Flores made the following statement: "Even with full-time work, almost half the people on the west side are living in poverty. San Antonio does not need alms and welfare. San Antonio needs just wages."

Ernesto Galarza (b. 1905) is one of many Mexican-American scholars who made significant contributions to American education. Known as the "dean of Chicano letters" and the "grandfather of the Chicano movement," Galarza has been dedicated to the promotion of bilingual and progressive education. Galarza is a prolific writer, and one of his most important works, *Merchants of Labor*, tells the story of the bracero program.

Mexican-American educator Lupe Anguiano (b. 1929) has been a nun, a teacher, and a social activist. Her work led her to a post with the De-

Ernesto Galarza has documented Mexican-American society in seven books.

partment of Health, Education and Welfare; her achievements included the organization of a Mexican-American division and development of the Bilingual Education Act. However, Anguiano became frustrated when bilingual program monies were used to fund remedial language programs that ignored students' native languages. This frustra-

San Antonio mayor Henry Cisneros was formerly a professor of urban studies.

tion led to her resignation, but it did not dampen her enthusiasm to work for social change. Anguiano worked closely with César Chávez and the farm workers movement, and in 1971 she returned to HEW's education branch to work as a civil rights specialist.

In 1981 Henry Cisneros (b. 1947) became the first Mexican-American mayor of a major U.S. city, San Antonio, Texas. He was reelected in 1983 and 1985. A popular political figure in Texas, Cisneros has served on a number of state and national committees and has received many awards and honors, including the Jefferson Award from the American Institute for Public Service and the Harvard Foundation Award for Contributions to American Cities and Politics. Rapidly gaining national attention, Cisneros will likely remain a prominent political figure for years to come.

Artists

Mexican-American artists have been influenced by both Spanish and Indian traditions. Two distinctly Mexican-American art forms are the mural and its pop counterpart, graffiti. The murals of the Chicano Renaissance (a movement that paralleled the Chicano Movement) reflect the Mexican muralist tradition. They often depict scenes from the Chicano experience. Because they are meant to be "art for the people," the murals are not confined to galleries and museums. These large paintings decorate the walls of public buildings, recreational areas, and schools, both inside and out. Chicano graffiti, a pop art companion to the mural, reveals a public pride in the strength of the Hispanic community. But Mexican Americans have also mastered more traditional Western art forms.

Octavio Medellin (b. 1907), whose family immigrated from Mexico to Texas, became interested in art and turned to primitive Indian crafts for inspiration. As a result, his strong, sensual sculptures reflect many pre-Columbian elements. He has worked and taught primarily in the Southwest, but his art is known throughout the world.

The landscape paintings of Porfirio Salinas (1910–1973), which record the beauty of the Southwest, have made him a celebrated Texas artist. With only three years of formal schooling, Salinas was essentially self-taught. His first real break came when Senator Sam Rayburn of Texas pur-

Images of the Chicano experience are not confined to museums and galleries.

Pancho Gonzáles proved that Mexican Americans could break into traditionally elite sports.

chased one of his paintings and took it back to Washington, D.C. It was not long before Salinas became the favorite artist of President Lyndon B. Johnson and began receiving widespread recognition for his work.

Writers

Many Mexican-American writers have played an important role in bringing the Chicano world into sharper view. For example, playwright Luis Valdez (b. 1940) and his *El Teatro Campesino* (The Farm Workers Theater) contributed largely to the cultural awakening of the Southwest. The group's inspiration sprang from the United Farm Workers Union conflicts that initiated the 1965 Delano, California, grape pickers' strike.

Under Valdez's direction, farm workers entertained the strikers and supporters with short skits. Using the vineyards as a stage and farm workers as actors and technicians, the wandering troupe performed from coast to coast, raising the political and social consciousness of its audiences. The Sleepy Lagoon case inspired Luis Valdez to write the play *Zoot Suit*, which in 1979 became the first Chicano play to appear on Broadway. El Teatro Campesino received critical acclaim, sparking the growth of similar theater companies throughout the Southwest.

Texas-born author Rolando Hinojosa-Smith (b. 1929) is another celebrated Mexican-American writer, who in 1972 received the prestigious Quinto Sol Prize for a collection of short prose pieces entitled *Estampas del Valle y Otras Obras* (The Valley and Other Stories). In 1976, when the Cuban publisher La Casa de Las Americas gave Hinojosa's *Klail City y Sus Alrededores* (Klail City and Its Surroundings) its award for the best novel of the year, international attention was focused on Mexican-American literature.

Much of the poetry published by Mexican-American poets in the last two decades has celebrated the group's ethnic identity. The poems of Alberto Alurista (b. 1947), which appear in many literary anthologies, reveal the poet's pride in his Mexican and Indian heritage. His poems ring with the barrio's rhythms as they move from English to Spanish and back again. His 1971 poetry collection, *Floricanto en Aztlán*, secures his place in the Chicano art world.

Sports Figures and Entertainers

Tennis star Richard "Pancho" Gonzáles (b. 1928) is considered one of the greatest tennis players of the 20th century. The winner of the U.S. Open in 1948 and 1949 and the Wimbledon doubles crown (with Frank Parker) in 1949, Gonzáles is probably the only self-taught tennis champion of modern times. Twenty years after his tennis debut, Gonzáles was still beating much younger competitors and had an audience appeal that has been compared to that of Babe Ruth.

Dallas-born champion golfer Lee Trevino (b. 1939) was named Sportsman of the Year in 1971 when he became one of the few golfers to win the United States Open and British Open championships in the same year. Nancy López (b. 1957) is having similar success in her golf career. The Associated Press named López Athlete of the Year in 1978. That same year, she was honored as Player and Rookie of the Year by the Ladies Professional Golf Association. Since then, López has won enough tournament championships to earn her a place in the LPGA Hall of Fame.

Singer Vikki Carr (b. 1941) was born Florencia Bisenta de Casillas Martínez Cardona. When a militant Mexican-American group confronted her about the name change, Carr explained that it was a matter of convenience. She also assured the group that she always tells the audience *exactly* who she is within the first five minutes of a performance. Carr also uses her gift for social causes. She has performed at numerous benefits and established a college scholarship fund for young Mexican Americans who show talent in the performing arts.

Folk singer and political activist Joan Baez (b. 1941) is the daughter of Mexican-born physicist Albert Baez. Joan had always excelled in music, and when her family moved to Boston her interest in folk music blossomed. She became influenced by the amateur folk musicians who entertained in Boston's many coffeehouses.

Baez identified with the social and political nature of folk music and gained international recognition in the turbulent 1960s. She was at the forefront of the anti–Vietnam War movement, the civil rights movement, and the farm workers movement. She founded the Institute for the Study of Nonviolence, and she also works for Amnesty International. In the summer of 1985, Baez brought her crusade for a better world to a new generation of Americans when she opened the Live Aid concert in Philadelphia to raise money for starving Ethiopians.

Actor Ricardo Montalbán (b. 1928), one of Hollywood's handsomest leading men, has received critical praise for his work on Broadway. In 1969 Montalbán founded and became the first president of Nosotros, an organization "dedicated to solving the injustices and problems involved in the hiring of Spanish-surnamed actors, actresses, and technicians in the motion picture and television industry." In recent years Montalbán starred as Mr. Rourke on television's "Fantasy Island." He is also known for his portrayal of space villain Khan Noonian Singh in Star Trek II: *The Wrath of Khan*.

Actor Anthony Rudolph Oaxaca Quinn (b. 1915) has starred in more than 100 films and has won two Oscars and several Academy Award nominations. However, he is best known for his portrayal of Zorba in both the play and the film versions of *Zorba the Greek*. In 1971, at the request of the United States Equal Employment Opportunity Commission, Quinn donated several weeks of his time to the Mexican-American cause by narrating and coproducing the documentary *The Voice of La Raza*. Its theme is the plight of Mexican Americans and Puerto Ricans in the United States. Quinn's 1972 autobiography, *The Original Sin: A Self-Portrait*, discusses his Mexican roots. ❧

Anthony Quinn was born in Chihuahua, Mexico in 1915.

Mexican-American men relax in a Santa Fe plaza.

THE STORY CONTINUES

Today's Mexican immigrants find a different America than their predecessors found. The Chicano Movement has ushered in a new sense of pride, as Chicanos have made a commitment to preserve their culture and to work for social change. The goals of Mexican-American leaders were best summed up by educator Lupe Anguiano in a speech that echoed the famous words of Martin Luther King, Jr.:

I have a dream. It is to see the realization of social change in this country in the area of accepting the language and culture of others. We shouldn't try to set up one culture as the one and only one. We should erase the aversion to nonconformity.

Although progress has been made, problems still exist. One of the most complex issues facing the U.S. and Mexican governments has been the increasing number of illegal aliens in the United States. Like the nativists (those who favor the native inhabitants) of a century ago, some argue that undocumented aliens take jobs away from U.S. citizens. Others believe that American employers have taken advantage of desperate Mexicans who

An American customs inspector at the U.S.-Mexico border asks visitors for proof of citizenship.

RESIDENT ALIEN

U.S. Department of Justice-Immigration and Naturalization Service

GARCIA-LOPEZ, ROSA MARIA

052356

A33500000

LOS NP1

The U.S. Immigration and Naturalization service now provides all registered aliens with cards that include a photograph, fingerprint, and biographical information.

will work for less than minimum wage and that Mexicans' willingness to work for meager wages dampened American industry's interest in relocating abroad in order to take advantage of a cheaper labor force.

Congress made an effort to resolve the problem of illegal aliens when it passed the Immigration Reform Act of 1986 and thereby subjected employers to fines ranging from $250 to $10,000 for each illegal alien they hire. The act grants amnesty to illegal aliens who can prove that they have lived in the United States since January 1, 1982. This provision may benefit millions of people. (However, many may find it difficult to establish the necessary proof because they have been in hiding for so long.) Congress also earmarked $4 billion to help defray increased schooling and social service costs for the newly legalized aliens.

The momentum to pass this bill, which had been stalled in Congress since 1982, grew in 1986, when Mexico's deteriorating economy increased the flow of illegal aliens across the Rio Grande. United States border officials expected to appre-

Hispanics and Anglos celebrate the San Antonio fiesta together at the Battle of Flowers Parade.

hend approximately 1.8 million illegal aliens in 1986—500,000 more than in 1985. Unfortunately, critics of the bill now fear that fines will discourage even sympathetic employers from hiring any citizens of Hispanic descent.

By the 1990s the United States will probably have the third-largest Spanish-speaking population in the world. In fact, during the 21st century, Hispanics will probably become the largest minority group in the United States. (In 1978, the U.S. Census Bureau estimated that the Mexican-American population exceeded 7.2 million.) This will undoubtedly change America. In the words of San Antonio's mayor, Henry Cisneros:

We have the opportunity here to create Hispanics who have developed the American virtues of hard work, discipline, and decisiveness while retaining their traditional values of the extended family, deep religious faith, and that innate sense of compassion which makes politics creative. There is also the opportunity here for developing a new breed of Anglos who take on the Hispanic qualities of tolerance, compassion, and appreciation for human relations. In other words, we have the potential to make *e pluribus unum* really mean something. ❧

Further Reading

Galarza, Ernesto. *Barrio Boy*. South Bend, IN: University of Notre Dame Press, 1971.

Meier, Matt S., and Feliciano Rivera, eds. *Dictionary of Mexican American History*. Westport, CT: Greenwood Press, 1981.

Meyer, Michael C., and William L. Sherman. *The Course of Mexican History*. 2nd ed. New York: Oxford University Press, 1983.

Moore, Joan W. *Mexican Americans*. 2d ed. Englewood Cliffs, NJ: Prentice Hall, 1970.

Moquin, Wayne, and Charles Van Doren. *A Documentary History of the Mexican Americans*. New York: Praeger, 1971.

Samora, Julian, and Patricia Vendel Simon. *A History of the Mexican-American People*. South Bend, IN: University of Notre Dame Press, 1977.

ACKNOWLEDGMENTS

Cover photo courtesy of *The San Antonio Light Collection*, Institute of Texan Cultures

We would like to thank the following sources for providing photographs: AFL-CIO, George Meany Archives: p. 62; American Friends Service Committee/Terry Foss: p. 60; American Museum of Natural History: p. 18; Bettmann Newsphotos: pp. 39, 40 (bottom); *A Child's History of the United States:* p. 22; Cityarts Workshop, Inc.: p. 38; Columbia Pictures Industries, Inc.: p. 83; Thomas W. Cutrer, copy courtesy Institute of Texan Cultures: p. 30; The Detroit Institute of Arts, Dirk Bakker, Chief Photographer: p. 36; Fiesta San Antonio Commission, Inc.: pp. 71 (Al Rendon), 88 (Gary Perkins); Howard Gale, U. S. Customs Service: p. 86; Robert Gumpert: p. 40 (top); Stewart Harvey: p. 84; Immigration and Naturalization Service: p. 87; La Fonda Hotel, Santa Fe, NM: p. 72; Library of Congress: pp. 14, 16, 29, 46, 55, 56, 59, 64; LA Mural Project: p. 79; the Mayor's Office, City of San Antonio, TX: p. 77; Mexican Government Tourist Office: pp. 34 (bottom), 73; New York Public Library Picture Collection: pp. 26, 80; New York Public Library Picture Collection/Joseph E. Smith: p. 42; Organization of American States: pp. 20, 25, 41; PAR/NYC: pp. 19, 34 (top); P. Harmon Parkhurst, courtesy of Museum of New Mexico: pp. 15, 66; Mrs. Robert Rubio, copy courtesy Institute of Texan Cultures: p. 68; *The San Antonio Light Collection*, Institute of Texan Cultures: pp. 49, 69; State of New Mexico, Office of the Governor: p. 65; State Records Center: p. 63; John L. Stoddard's Lectures: pp. 21, 27; Ida Trevino, copy courtesy Institute of Texan Cultures: p. 44; UPI/Bettmann Newsphotos: pp. 50, 53, 74; University of Notre Dame Press: p. 76; Laurie Platt Winfrey, Inc.: pp. 12, 33, 35. Photo Research: PAR/NYC.

JULIE CATALANO, a writer from San Antonio, Texas, has contributed articles on politics, culture, and the arts to local and national magazines and newspapers.

DANIEL PATRICK MOYNIHAN is the senior United States senator from New York. He is also the only person in American history to serve in the cabinets or subcabinets of four successive presidents—Kennedy, Johnson, Nixon, and Ford. Formerly a professor of government at Harvard University, he has written and edited many books, including *Beyond the Melting Pot, Ethnicity: Theory and Experience* (both with Nathan Glazer), *Loyalties,* and *Family and Nation.*